Core Knowledge Language Arts®

Unit 2
Workbook

Skills Strand
GRADE 2

Amplify learning.

Core Knowledge®

ISBN 978-1-61700-220-5

© 2013 Core Knowledge Foundation
www.coreknowledge.org

Printed in the USA
NA03 RROW 2016

Unit 2
Workbook

This Workbook contains worksheets that accompany the lessons from the Teacher Guide for Unit 2. Each worksheet is identified by its page number. Some of the worksheets in this book do not include written instructions for the student because the instructions would have contained undecodable words. The expectation is teachers will explain these worksheets to students orally using the guidelines in the Teacher Guide. The Workbook is a student component, which means each student should have a Workbook.

Dear Family Member,

We have started a new Reader called *Bedtime Tales*. It is an ongoing story of a little boy named Mike who doesn't want to go to bed at bedtime. Does this sound familiar to you? Mike is persuaded to go to bed by his dad telling him bedtime stories. We hope your child will enjoy this series of stories and you will also enjoy telling some bedtime tales to your child. Telling and reading stories at bedtime are valuable ways to improve you child's vocabulary and future school success.

You will see the spelling words for this week below. As always, please practice these words with your child each night. Call out the words and ask your child to write them down. Alternately, you could ask your child to copy each word three times.

Root Word	Suffix	**Spelling Word**
yell	-ed	**yelled**
yank	-ed	**yanked**
slump	-ed	**slumped**
limp	-ed	**limped**
plop	-ed	**plopped**
smile	-ed	**smiled**
shrug	-ed	**shrugged**
like	-ed	**liked**
pat	-ed	**patted**

Tricky Word: you

gave	drive	smile	like	cake

1. Mike _____ Dad a hot dog.

2. "Let's go for a _____," said Dad.

3. "Would you _____ to go to the zoo?" asked Dad.

4. "Yes," said Mike with a _____.

5. "I like the _____ best," Dad said.

slid_____   slim_____   plan_____

grim_____   spin_____   mad_____

pin_____   glad_____   quit_____

Jan_____   Sam_____   twin_____

fat_____   sit_____   win_____

rip_____   fad_____   hid_____

Mike's Bedtime

1. How old is Mike?

   A. 6

   B. 7

   C. 8

   Page _____

2. It was _____ black.

   A. catch

   B. watch

   C. pitch

   Page _____

3. What did Mike yank back?

   A. Mike yanked back the cakes.

   B. Mike yanked back the drapes.

   C. Mike yanked back the capes.

   Page _____

4. If the sun is down and the street lamp is on, what time is it?

_____

_____

_____

Page _____

5. Why did Mike make a face?

_____

_____

_____

Page _____

6. What will Mike's dad do?

_____

_____

_____

Page _____

Directions: 1) Teacher reads the word. 2) Student writes letter 'e' on word. 3) Teacher says, "Alakazam!" 4) All students read the new word.

cub____   slop____   us____

hop____   not____   cut____

cop____   fat____   slid____

pop____   rob____   wok____

mop____   tap____   cub____

1. tadpole

2. bathrobe

3. trombone

4. remote

5. backbone

6. foxhole

7. rosebud

8. hopeful

9. compute

10. confuse

11. conclude

12. dispute

13. rosebush

Directions: Ask students to read the words and horseshoe circle the letters that make the /oe/ and /ue/ sounds.

Dear Family Member,

Ask your child to read the words aloud to you. Then ask your child to horseshoe circle the letters that make the /oe/ and /ue/ sounds. Next, ask your child to use the words in the box to complete the sentences

hope	cute	note	rope
poke	broke	shone	huge

1. Can you lift a _____ block?

2. The sun _____ on the rock.

3. I _____ I can get a ride.

4. The cup _____ when it dropped.

5. Did you _____ him in the side?

6. Let's jump _____!

7. My _____ pup is tan and black.

8. I will write a _____ to mom.

Directions: Students should write at least four sentences in response to the prompt: By the end of the tale, what did Jane learn?

Name _____

Dear Family Member:

Your child read this story in class earlier this week. Please ask your child to read the story aloud to you.

The Milk

Mike's dad was getting set to tell a bedtime tale. He said, "The name of this bedtime tale is *The Milk.*"

Once upon a time, a lass named Jane set off from home to sell a bucket of milk.

As she went, she was thinking of the cash she would get from selling the milk.

"I have big plans. I will sell this milk," she said, "and I will use the cash to get a hen. I hope my hen will make lots of eggs."

"Then I will sell those eggs and use the cash to get a cute piglet.

I will take care of the piglet and let him munch on pig slop till he gets nice and plump."

"Then I will sell the pig and get a nice dress that I can dance in, and . . ."

But just as she was thinking of the dress, she tripped on a stone and the bucket fell with a crash. The milk splashed on the path. Jane made a face and fumed at the spilt milk.

Moral: Take one step at a time.

"Is that the end?" asked Mike.

"That's it," said his dad.

"What a shame!" said Mike. "She had such big plans!"

Mike's dad nodded. "You can make plans, but planning by itself will not make things happen."

Mike sat thinking a bit. Then he said, "Dad, that bedtime tale was not bad. But it was sad. Next time would you tell a fun tale?"

"Yes," said his dad. "Next time."

Can you tell a fun tale?

Mike asked, _____

_____

_____

_____

I don't like beets.

Jane said, _____

_____

_____

_____

A stream is nice.

Ann said, _____

_____

_____

_____

Beans are fun to pick.

Dad said, _____

_____

_____

_____

The Jumping Frog

Directions: Ask students to find the best answer to each question. Students should record the page number where the answer is found.

1. Big Jim bragged that his frog had _____.

    A. spunk.

    B. speed.

    C. three legs.

    Page _____

2. How much cash did Big Jim bet on his frog?

    A. He bet one buck.

    B. He bet five bucks.

    C. He bet ten bucks.

    Page _____

3. Why did Big Jim run to the stream?

    A. Big Jim ran to the stream to catch a frog for Pete.

    B. Big Jim ran to the stream to set his frog free.

    C. Big Jim ran to the stream to swim.

    Page _____

4. Who held Big Jim's frog while he ran off to the stream?

    A. Big Jim's mom held his frog.

    B. Big Jim held the frog.

    C. Pete held Big Jim's frog.

    Page _____

5. What does it mean to bet?

_____

_____

_____

_____

Page _____

6. Why didn't Mike's dad finish the tale?

_____

_____

_____

_____

Page _____

7. Predict what will happen next in the story.

_____

_____

_____

_____

TAKE HOME

Directions: Draw a picture about the story "The Jumping Frog," and write a sentence about the picture.

Spelling Test

1. _____

2. _____

3. _____

4. _____

5. _____

6. _____

7. _____

8. _____

9. _____

10. _____

 _____

_____

1. A stove can drool. _____

2. A big lake can be nice. _____

3. We stood in line to get shampoo. _____

4. A pool is a good place to plant seeds. _____

5. Brooms can hop. _____

6. Ice is needed to heat a woodstove. _____

7. A sheep can say, "Moo."_____

8. A frog likes to be by a stream. _____

9. I can wave my hand to shoo a bug. _____

Directions: Have students write 'yes' or 'no' beside each sentence.

Dear Family Member,

This week during our language arts time, we will begin to explore the writing process with students. Students will learn to plan, draft, and edit their work before creating a final product. We will not "publish" each piece of writing that we create. From time to time, we will select pieces to publish. In the meantime, you will see writing coming home in backpacks. Ask your child to explain the process to you. At home, you can help by suggesting your child write simple notes for you.

Your child will only be tested on the words in the third column marked "Spelling Word." Please note that for these words, the final 'e' is dropped and replaced with -*ing*.

Root Word	Suffix	**Spelling Word**
smile	-ing	**smiling**
race	-ing	**racing**
hope	-ing	**hoping**
bake	-ing	**baking**
invite	-ing	**inviting**
confuse	-ing	**confusing**
taste	-ing	**tasting**
compete	-ing	**competing**
hop	-ing	**hopping**

Tricky Word: were

Title:

Characters

Setting

Plot

Beginning

Middle

End

Editing Checklist

Ask yourself these questions as you edit your draft.

1. Do I have a title?	
2. Have I described the setting at the start?	
3. Have I named and described the characters?	
4. Do I have a plot with • a beginning? • a middle? • an end?	
5. Do all of my sentences start with uppercase letters?	
6. Do all of my sentences end with a final mark? (. ? or !)	
7. Have I spelled all of my words correctly?	
8. Have I added "sense" words that describe how things look, feel, taste, sound, or smell?	

doing	enjoying	giving	writing	hoping	~~baking~~

1. Mom asked, Would you like to join me in ____baking____

    a cake?

2. Jane said, Yes, Mom, I am _____ I can lick the bowl.

3. Mom asked, Are you _____ your time with Mike?

4. Jane said, I will be _____ him a bit of cake.

5. Mom asked, What have you been _____ at

    school?

6. Jane said, We have been reading and _____.

Dear Family Member:

This is the second part of a trickster tale that we are reading in class. In the first part, Big Jim wagers that he has the fastest frog in the West. A stranger named Pete shows up to accept the wager. Below you will find the conclusion of the story.

The Frog Race

"Dad," Mike said when he woke up, "what happened with the jumping frog? I missed the end of the tale. I was sleeping."

"I did not tell it to the end," said his dad. "When you drifted off to sleep, I stopped."

"Oh, tell the ending!" said Mike.

Mike's dad picked up the tale where he had left off.

Big Jim handed his frog to Pete and ran off to the stream.

Pete held Big Jim's frog in his hand. Pete looked at the frog. Then Pete reached into his pocket and got a pile of limes. Yum—Big Jim's frog drooled. The frog ate the whole pile of limes from Pete's hand! Then Pete set the frog down.

While Pete was feeding the frog limes, Big Jim was down at the stream. He tossed off his boots and went frog hunting. At last he nabbed a nice green frog. He ran back and handed the frog to Pete.

"There's your frog!" said Jim. "Just set him down there next to my frog. Then we will let them compete to see which one of them is the fastest!"

Pete set his frog down.

"All set?" said Jim.

"All set," said the man.

Then Jim yelled, "Jump, frogs, jump!"

Pete gave the two frogs a tap to get them jumping. His frog hopped off nice and quick. But Jim's frog just sat there. Once he hitched up his legs like he was fixing to jump. But it was no use. With all those limes in him, he was planted there just as solid as a rock. His tummy was full!

Pete's frog hopped and hopped till it got to the finish line.

"Fine race!" said Pete. He took Jim's ten bucks and slipped the cash in his pocket. Then Pete tipped his hat and set off.

Well, Big Jim was stunned. "What happened to my frog?" he said. "I hope he's not sick."

He bent down and picked up the frog and rubbed his tummy.

"Goodness!" said Jim. "He must have had a big lunch!"

"I think Pete tricked me! He fed my frog too much to eat!" Jim said. Big Jim let out a whoop. His face got red. Jim ran to catch Pete. But it was no use. Pete had run off. Pete had tricked Big Jim!

_____

_____ said Mike.

_____

_____ said Jane.

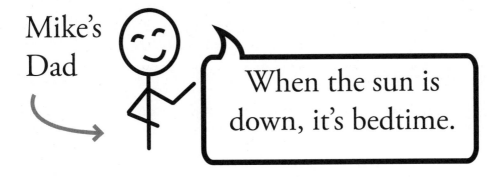

_____

_____ said Mike's Dad.

Directions: Have students write the sentence from the bubble on the line with quoation marks.

Spell the word. Then print it on the line.

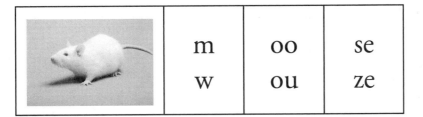	h w	oo ou	se ze

_____

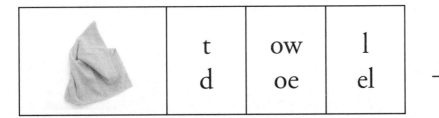	m w	oo ou	se ze

_____

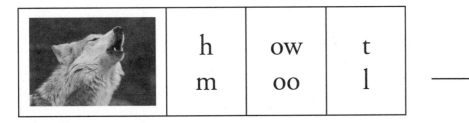	h m	ow oo	t l

_____

	t d	ow oe	l el

_____

	c s	t r	ow ou	n m

_____

	c s	oi oe	t n	z s	_____
	c s	l w	ee e	r p	_____
	ch sh	e oe	l ll	f p	_____
	p b	t r	oo u	n m	_____
	k c	r wr	ow oy	ed d	_____

The Hare and the Hedgehog

1.   Why was the hare proud?

    A.   He was fast.

    B.   He was funny.

    C.   He was nice.

    Page _____

2. What did the hedgehog ask the hare to do after lunch?

    A.   The hedgehog asked the hare to take a nap.

    B.   The hedgehog asked the hare to race.

    C.   The hedgehog asked the hare to run home.

    Page _____

3. Tell the plot of this tale. Write 3-4 sentences.

    _____

    _____

    _____

    _____

    _____

    _____

    Page _____

Spelling Test

1. _____

2. _____

3. _____

4. _____

5. _____

6. _____

7. _____

8. _____

9. _____

10. _____

 _____

_____

'er' > /er/ (*her*)

Directions: Have students find and circle the word with the 'er' spelling in each sentence. On the line below, have students write the word and circle the 'er' spelling.

1. Last summer was hot.

    _____

2. Who is that person?

    _____

3. The water is so cold!

    _____

4. The book is under the bed.

    _____

5. My mother's name is Ann.

    _____

'er' > /er/ (*her*)

| flower | never | river | after | later |

1. _____

   _____

2. _____

   _____

3. _____

   _____

4. _____

   _____

5. _____

   _____

Directions: Have students create sentences with the words containing the 'er' spelling.

How the Hedgehog Tricked the Hare

1. The hedgehog made a _____ to trick the hare.

   A.   plan

   B.   tale

   C.   race

   Page _____

2. The hedgehog and the hare lined up to race at _____.

   A.   the well

   B.   the fence

   C.   the house

   Page _____

3. Next the hare ran past _____.

   A.   the well

   B.   the fence

   C.   the house

   Page _____

4. The hare ran up to _____.

   A.   the well

   B.   the fence

   C.   the house

   Page _____

5. Why did the hare run to the fence and back ten times?

_____

_____

_____

_____

_____

Page _____

6. Why did the hedgehog smile in the end?

_____

_____

_____

_____

_____

Page _____

Dear Family Member,

These are our spelling words for this week. The spellings words on which your child will be tested are the contractions listed in the second column, plus the one Tricky Word. When practicing spelling contractions this week with your child, please also review the two words that form the contraction. For example, one way to practice would be to say two words, e.g., *it is*, and then ask your child to write the contraction, e.g., *it's*.

Your child is also bringing home a story to read, "How the Hedgehog Tricked the Hare," and an accompanying worksheet. We have been discussing in class the characters, setting, and plot for each story. After reading the story, your child will complete a worksheet and identify the characters, setting, and plot. You can encourage your child to look back at the story to find the answers. **This worksheet will be used to help your child write a book report about the story, so please make sure your child completes and bring this homework back to school tomorrow.**

	Spelling Word
it is	**it's**
that is	**that's**
she is	**she's**
is not	**isn't**
are not	**aren't**
was not	**wasn't**
I will	**I'll**
you will	**you'll**
she will	**she'll**

Tricky Word: their

How the Hedgehog Tricked the Hare

"Where was it I left off?" asked Mike's dad.

"The hedgehog was telling his wife the plan to trick the hare," said Mike.

"Got it!" said his dad.

The hedgehog made a map of his plan. He pointed to the map and outlined his plan to trick the hare.

"The hare and I will race from down by the fence up to the house on the hill," the hedgehog said to his wife. "I need you to stand next to the house. Stand in a spot where the hare can't see you. And be on the lookout, my dear!"

The hedgehog's wife nodded and said, "Your map is clear. I will be there."

The hedgehog went on, "When the hare gets close, you must pop out and shout, 'There you are! What took you so long?' But when you do this, make your voice deep and stern like my voice. The hare can't tell one hedgehog from the next. If you sound like me, he will think you are me. And he will think that he has lost the race!"

"What a clever plan!" said his wife. "It's perfect!"

She puckered up and kissed him on one of his cheeks, where he had no spikes. The hedgehog handed his wife the map.

After his meal, the hedgehog went to the fence. His wife went up to the house on the hill.

The hedgehog and the hare lined up.

"All set?" said the hare.

"All set," said the hedgehog.

"Run!" said the hare.

The hare bounded off. He was a fast and powerful runner. In a flash he ran down the hill, past the well, and up to the house.

When he got to the top of the hill, there was a hedgehog standing next to the house.

It was the hedgehog's wife, but she spoke in a deep, stern voice like a male hedgehog. "There you are!" she said. "What took you so long?"

The hare was stunned. "It can't be!" he said. "How did you get here so fast? I will race you back to the fence!"

And so the hare ran back past the well and up the hill until he got back to the fence.

And what did he see when he got there?

A hedgehog! This time it was the male hedgehog. The hedgehog said, "There you are! What took you so long?"

"No, no, no!" screamed the hare. The hare lost his temper. "It can't be. It can't be. I am faster. I will race you back to the house! You can't beat me!"

So the hare ran back up the hill, past the well, and up to the house.

And what did he see when he got there?

A hedgehog! This time it was the hedgehog's wife. In a deep, stern voice, she said, "There you are! What took you so long?"

The hare ran to the fence and back ten times. But it was the same all ten times. At last he was so tired out that he fell on the ground next to the male hedgehog. He could not stop huffing and puffing. He frowned and said, with a gasp, "I feel weak. You are faster and better than me!"

The hedgehog just smiled.

Reminder: Bring back to school tomorrow.

Title:

Characters	Setting

Directions: Complete the worksheet after reading "How the Hedgehog Tricked the Hare."

Plot

Beginning

Middle

End

park	car	short	shower	shark

Directions: In the word box, have students circle the spelling of either 'or' or 'ar' in the words. Next, ask students to write the words in the appropriate sentence.

1. We like to go to the _____ to eat a picnic lunch.

2. Kate is not tall. She is _____.

3. We had a rain _____.

4. The _____ is red and fast.

5. A _____ is in the sea.

sports	flower	fork	dark	barking

6. I need a _____ to eat my food.

7. The dog will not stop _____!

8. Do you enjoy _____ like soccer?

9. The _____ smells nice.

10. The lamp is on since it is _____

and hard to see.

Quotation Marks

1. our dog likes to bark said Roy

_____

_____

_____

2. james asked is this game fun

_____

_____

_____

3. troy asked can we go to the park

_____

_____

_____

4. i hope we can go to the park after lunch said Nate

_____

_____

_____

5. hand the flower pot to Jane said Mike

_____

_____

_____

6. deb said this is a fast game

_____

_____

_____

Title _____

The main characters are _____

_____

_____

_____

_____

The tale takes place _____

_____

_____

_____

In the tale (plot) _____

_____

_____

_____

_____

_____

_____

_____

Directions: Have students use the template for their book reports.

Tell how you can tell "The Pancake, Part I" is a made-up tale.

_____

- -

_____

- -

_____

- -

_____

- -

_____

- -

_____

- -

_____

Name _____

TAKE HOME

Dear Family Member:

This is the first part of a trickster tale we are reading in class. Please ask your child to read it aloud to you.

The Pancake, Part I

"Did you enjoy the tale of the hedgehog and the hare?" asked Mike's dad.

"Yes, I liked it," said Mike. "The hedgehog came up with a good trick."

"The tale I'd like to tell you next has a trick in it, too."

"Cool!" said Mike. "Is there a hedgehog in it?"

"Nope," said his dad. "But there is a pancake in it!"

"A pancake?"

"Yep."

"Neat! Tell it!"

"But the sun has not set yet! The street lamp is not on yet!"

"Please! I would like to hear it! Will you tell the pancake tale!"

Once upon a time there was a mom who had six kids. One morning the mom was grilling a pancake for the kids. The

kids looked at the pancake. They got out their forks and started licking their lips.

The pancake looked back at the kids. He was scared. He feared the kids would eat him. When the mom was not looking, the pancake jumped out of the pan and ran off.

The pancake ran out of the house.

"Stop, pancake!" shouted the mom from the porch.

"Stop, pancake!" shouted the six kids.

All seven of them chased the pancake as he ran out of the yard.

But the pancake was too fast. He outran them all.

The pancake ran north on a foot path. He zoomed past a barn and two farmers who were plowing the ground.

"Why are you running, pancake?" the farmers asked.

The pancake shouted, "I've outrun a mom and six kids, and I can outrun you too! I'm too fast and too smart for you."

"You think so?" said the farmers. They started running. But the pancake was too fast. He outran the farmers.

Just then Mike's sister Ann came in. She was just three. She had on her gown for bed.

"Dad," she said, "will you tell it to me, too?"

"Yes, I will," said her dad. "You can sit up here with Mike and hear the rest of the tale."

Editing Checklist

Ask yourself these questions as you edit your draft.

1. Do I have a title?	
2. Have I described the setting at the start?	
3. Have I named and described the characters?	
4. Do I have a plot with • a beginning? • a middle? • an end?	
5. Do all of my sentences start with uppercase letters?	
6. Do all of my sentences end with a final mark? (. ? or !)	
7. Have I spelled all of my words correctly?	
8. Have I added "sense" words that describe how things look, feel, taste, sound, or smell?	

The Pancake, Part II

1. The pancake first ran past farmers. Then he ran past _____.

   A.   a fox

   B.   a hen

   C.   a pig

2. The pancake ran past a hen. As the hen chased the pancake, she was _____.

   A.   clucking

   B.   snorting

   C.   yelling

3. How did the fox trick the pancake?

   _____

   _____

   _____

   _____

   _____

   _____

   _____

   _____

   _____

   _____

Directions: Have students reread the story and answer the questions in complete sentences.

The Pancake, Part II

Directions: Have students number the sentences in the correct order using the story page numbers, then cut and paste them on Worksheet 13.4.

☐ The pancake ran past a fox. (Page ____)

☐ The fox ate the pancake. (Page ____)

☐ The pancake ran by a pig. (Page ____)

☐ The pancake shouted, "I'VE OUTRUN A MOM, SIX KIDS, TWO FARMERS, A PIG, AND A HEN, AND I CAN OUTRUN YOU, TOO! I AM TOO FAST AND SMART FOR YOU!" (Page____)

☐ The pancake ran by a hen. (Page ____)

The Pancake, Part II

1.

2.

3.

4.

5.

The Pancake, Part II

"Let's see," said Mike's dad. "Where did I stop?"

"The pancake was running," said Mike. "He had just outrun the two farmers."

"OK," said Mike's dad. "Let's start there."

The pancake ran on until, by and by, he ran past a pig.

"Why are you running, pancake?" the pig asked.

The pancake shouted, "I've outrun a mom, six kids, and two farmers, and I can outrun you too! I am too fast and too smart for you."

"You think so?" said the pig. Then it snorted and started running. The pig chased the pancake. But the pancake was too fast.

The pancake ran on until, by and by, he ran past a hen.

"Why are you running, pancake?" the hen asked.

The pancake shouted, "I've outrun a mom, six kids, two farmers, and a pig, and I can outrun you too! I am too fast and too smart for you."

"You think so?" said the hen. Then she set off, clucking as she ran. The hen chased the pancake. But the pancake was too fast.

The pancake went on until, by and by, he ran past a fox.

"Why are you running, pancake?" the fox asked.

The pancake said, "I've outrun a mom, six kids, two farmers, a pig, and a hen, and I can outrun you too! I am too fast and too smart for you!"

The fox did not get up. He just sat there and said, "What was that you said? I could not quite make it out."

The pancake stopped running and yelled, **"I've outrun a mom, six kids, two farmers, a pig, and a hen, and I can outrun you too! I am too fast and too smart for you!"**

The fox squinted and said, "What was that you said? I still could not quite hear you. Why do you stand so far off? Stand nearer to me so I can hear you."

The pancake ran up near to the fox. Then he shouted at the top of his lungs: **"I'VE OUTRUN A MOM, SIX KIDS, TWO FARMERS, A PIG, AND A HEN, AND I CAN OUTRUN YOU TOO! I AM TOO FAST AND TOO SMART FOR YOU!"**

"You think so?" said the fox. "I think you made a mistake and got a bit too close." Then he scooped the pancake into his mouth and ate it for dinner.

And that was the end of the pancake. And that is the end of the tale.

Antonyms

1	inside	bad	
2	soft	long	
3	add	cold	
4	good	rounded	
5	short	hard	
6	shout	subtract	
7	pointed	outside	1
8	hot	whisper	

Editing Checklist

Ask yourself these questions as you edit your draft.

1. Do I have a title?	
2. Have I described the setting at the start?	
3. Have I named and described the characters?	
4. Do I have a plot with • a beginning? • a middle? • an end?	
5. Do all of my sentences start with uppercase letters?	
6. Do all of my sentences end with a final mark? (. ? or !)	
7. Have I spelled all of my words correctly?	
8. Have I added "sense" words that describe how things look, feel, taste, sound, or smell?	

Spelling Test

1. _____

2. _____

3. _____

4. _____

5. _____

6. _____

7. _____

8. _____

9. _____

10. _____

 _____

_____

sick	visit	out
hare	cave	owl

The panther was _____. He could

not leave his _____. First the panther

said to the _____, "I am sick. Will you

_____ me in my cave?" The

owl went inside the cave, but he did not

step _____. Next the panther said to

the _____, "I am sick. Will you visit me

in my cave?" The hare went inside the cave, but he

did not step out.

Directions: Have students fill in the blanks with the best word choice from the box.

The tale I like the best from *Bedtime Tales* is:

_____

In the tale:

_____

_____

_____

_____

_____

_____

_____

The reasons I like this tale are:

_____

_____

_____

_____

_____

Draw a picture from this tale.

Mark the words that are said.

1. sitter   stern   sister   stinger

2. rate   rake   rat   ran

3. be   bet   beet   best

4. booking   bout   bake   book

5. here   there   theme   them

6. foil   foul   feel   fool

7. join   joint   joust   joyful

8. pork   park   perk   pick

9. fin   fine   five   fit

10. Bart   farm   port   part

11. cut   cute   cube   cull

12. hoop   hope   hop   hopping

13. jeep   germ   jerk   jeans

14. employ   joy   joyful   enjoy

15. bet   batch   beach   beet

16. clown   cow   crown   cloud

17. stern   seem   steam   stream

18. tout   tart   toot   foot

Cat and Mouse Keep House

1. Mike asked for a bedtime tale that had _____.

   A.   a trick

   B.   a dog

   C.   a joke

   Page _____

2. What did the cat and mouse set up?

   A.   The cat and mouse set up tricks.

   B.   The cat and mouse set up a mat.

   C.   The cat and mouse set up house.

   Page _____

3. What was in the jar?
   In the jar was _____.

   A.   some jam

   B.   a pancake

   C.   a smaller jar

   Page _____

4. Where did cat and mouse hide the jar?
   The cat and mouse hid the jar _____.

   A.   in a tree

   B.   in a bigger jar

   C.   in the house next door

   Page _____

Directions: Have students circle the letter next to the best answer to each question.

5.   Who went to eat the jam first?

_____

_____

_____

_____

Page _____

6.   Why did the mouse want to eat the jam?

_____

_____

_____

_____

Page _____

7.   The cat tricked the mouse. This made the mouse feel
     _____ at the cat.

  A.   mad

  B.   sad

  C.   scared

  Page _____

8.   What did the cat do to the mouse?

  A.   The cat sat on the mouse.

  B.   The cat ate the mouse.

  C.   The cat hid the mouse.

  Page _____

Name _____

Start time: _____

The Fox and the Cat

Once a fox and a cat were drinking from a river.   11

The fox started bragging.   15

"I am a clever one," said the fox. "There are lots of beasts out   29
there that would like to eat me, but they can't catch me. I have lots   60
of tricks that help me escape from them. I can run. I can swim. I can   60
dig a hole and hide. Why, I must have a hundred clever tricks!"   73

"I have just one trick," said the cat. "But it is a good one."   87

"Just one?" said the fox. "That's all? Well, that is too bad for   100
you!"   101

Just then there was a loud sound. It was the sound of barking   114
dogs. A hunter was leading a pack of hunting dogs by the side of the   129
river.   130

The cat scampered up a tree and hid in the leaves.   141

"This my plan," said the cat. "What are you going to do?"   153

The fox started thinking which of his tricks he should use.   164
Should he run? Should he swim? Should he dig a hole and hide? He   178
had such a long list of tricks. It was hard to pick just one. But while   194
he was thinking, the hunter and his dogs were getting nearer and   206
nearer. Soon they spotted the fox and then it was too late.   218

The cat said, "It's better to have one trick you can count on than   232
a hundred you can't."   236

Stop time: _____

Discussion Questions (note student's answers)

1.

2.

3.

4.

5.

6.

WCPM Calculation Worksheet

Student: _____

Date: _____

Story: *The Fox and the Cat*

Total words in story: 236

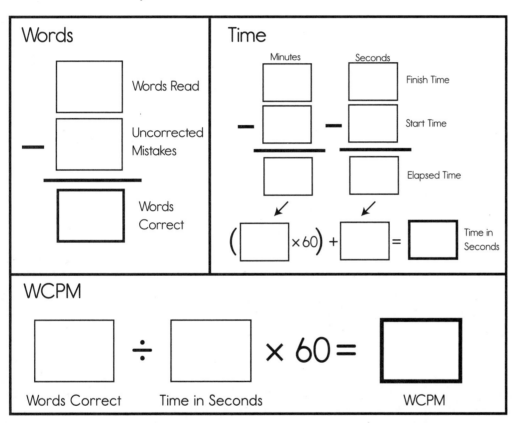

Compare the student's WCPM score to national norms for Fall of Grade 2 (Hasbrouck and Tindal, 2006):

    90th percentile: 106 WCPM

    75th percentile: 79 WCPM

    50th percentile: 51 WCPM

    25th percentile: 25 WCPM

    10th percentile: 11 WCPM

catch	green
spend	boil
trick	spoon
cord	foot
bunch	cloud
space	broil
lime	fern
slope	thorn
cute	yard

Directions: Have students read each word and circle the letter or letters for the vowel sound in the word.

finish	shortcut
after	shampoo
basement	downtown
footprint	priceless
wishbone	morning
bedtime	hillside
pavement	napping
sleeping	mushroom
discount	number

Count the sounds in the word. Write the number of sounds in the box. Print the word on the line.

1. cloud ☐4☐ _____cloud_____

2. grapes _____

3. twitch _____

4. foil _____

5. crow _____

6. short ☐ _____

7. teeth ☐ _____

8. joke ☐ _____

9. parking ☐ _____

10. choice ☐ _____

11. winter ☐ _____

Which word matches the picture? Write it on the line.

(grapes) gate

coin corn

grapes _____

_____

sleep slope

slide dive

_____

_____

| book cook | drive dive |

_____

_____

| short shark | home hill |

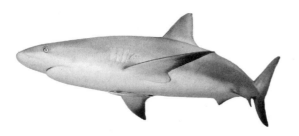

_____

_____

Name _____

Spell the word. Then print it on the line.

	(ar) r	(t) d	(i) c	k (s)	(t) f	artist

	h d	ar a	k p	_____

	p b	u ar	x k	_____

[Queen of hearts card]	qu k	oo ee	n m	_____

	b d	oo ou	t k	_____

	s c	p k	u oo	d n	_____
	kn k	e i	v f	i e	_____
	t f	ar or	d m	r er	_____
	p g	l w	o d	t b	e a	_____
	g c	ar r	m d	e o	n d	_____

Print the words on the lines where they fit the best. Use each word in a sentence.

1. fork

___fork___   _____

The fork is sharp. _____

_____

2. slide

_____   _____

_____

_____

3. coin

_____   _____

_____

_____

4. igloo

_____   _____

_____

_____

5. pancakes

_____   _____

_____

_____

6. rooster

_____   _____

_____

_____

Print the words in the box on the lines where they fit the best.

mule	cake	spoon
~~kite~~	house	tree

kite _____   _____   _____

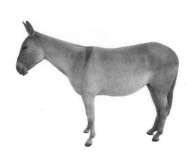

_____   _____   _____

coin	rope	hook
cloud	fern	vase

_____   _____   _____

_____   _____   _____

a_e = brown
i_e = orange

Directions: Ask students to read each word and to then color the spaces of words with /ae/ brown and the spaces of words with /ie/ orange.

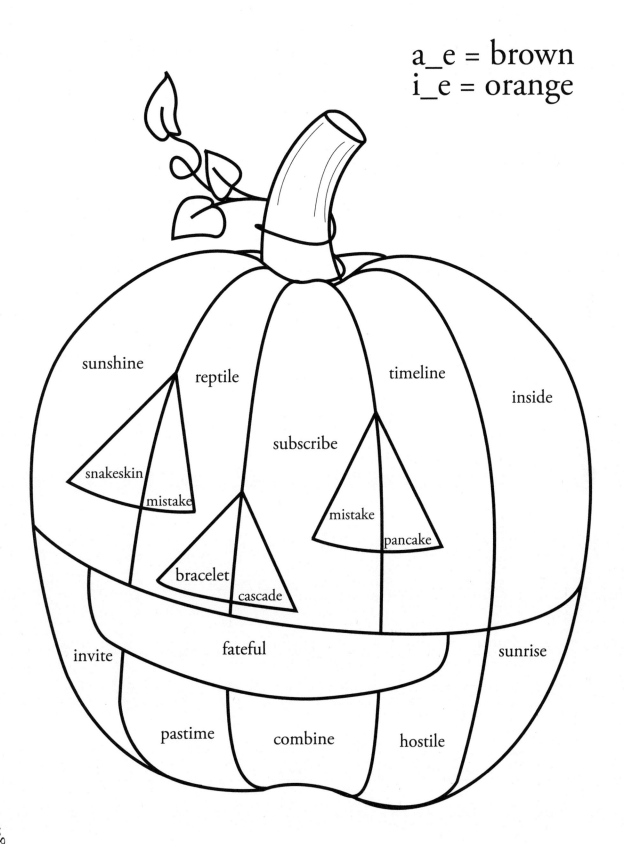

sunshine
reptile
timeline
inside
snakeskin
mistake
subscribe
mistake
pancake
bracelet
cascade
fateful
sunrise
invite
pastime
combine
hostile

m a d   →   m d e

___ ___ ___   ___ ___ ___ ___

___ ___ ___   ___ ___ ___ ___

___ ___ ___   ___ ___ ___ ___

   ___ ___ ___ ___

___ ___ ___   →   ___ ___ ___ ___

Directions: Have students write each word sound by sound as you pronounce each word.

1. fad   fade   fate   _____fade_____

2. slope   slop   sop   _____

3. cap   cope   cape   _____

4. joke   jock   jot   _____

5. dime   dim   dine   _____

6. cane   can   corn   _____

7. fake   fad   fade   _____

8. late   lad   lake   _____

9. mode   made   mad   _____

10. mute   moot   mate   _____

11. bit   bite   bike   _____

12. hop   hope   hoop   _____

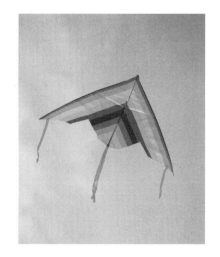

dim	kit	fin
dine	kite	find
dime	kiss	fine

rate	cute	pin
rake	cap	pint
rat	cut	pine

rod	cap	mate
rode	cane	mat
red	cape	male

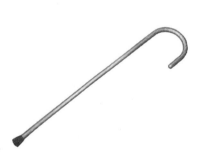

10		
ten	can	pale
teen	cane	pane
tent	cape	pan

Print the words in the box on the lines where they fit best.

lines	bike	gate
kite	~~nine~~	plate

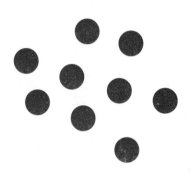

  n̅i̅n̅e̅
_____
_____
_____

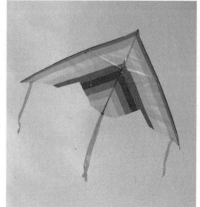

_____
_____
_____

Directions: Ask students to horeshoe-circle the separated digraphs in each word.

dime	cube	grapes
globe	cone	cake

_____

_____

_____

_____

_____

_____

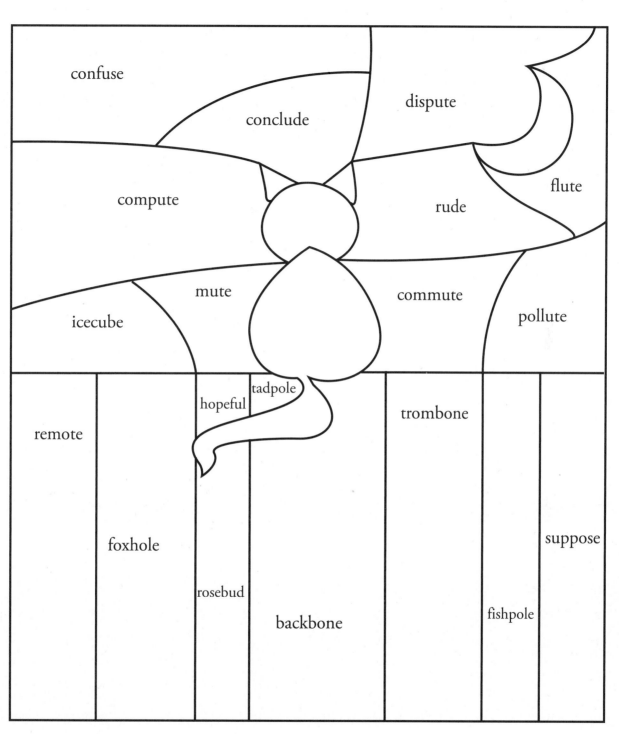

confuse

conclude

dispute

compute

flute

rude

mute

icecube

commute

pollute

hopeful

tadpole

remote

trombone

foxhole

rosebud

suppose

backbone

fishpole

Directions: Have students color the areas with /oe/ words light brown and /ue/ words blue.

/oe/ = light brown

/ue/ = blue

Print the words in the box on the lines where they fit best.

| bee | beans | leaf |
| peanuts | teacup | ~~seashell~~ |

seashell
_____   _____   _____

_____   _____   _____

| wheat | chimpanzee | eel |
| athlete | cheese | geese |

_____   _____   _____

_____   _____   _____

Directions: Ask students to read each word and circle only the words that have the /ee/ sound so Jane can follow the path to go back home.

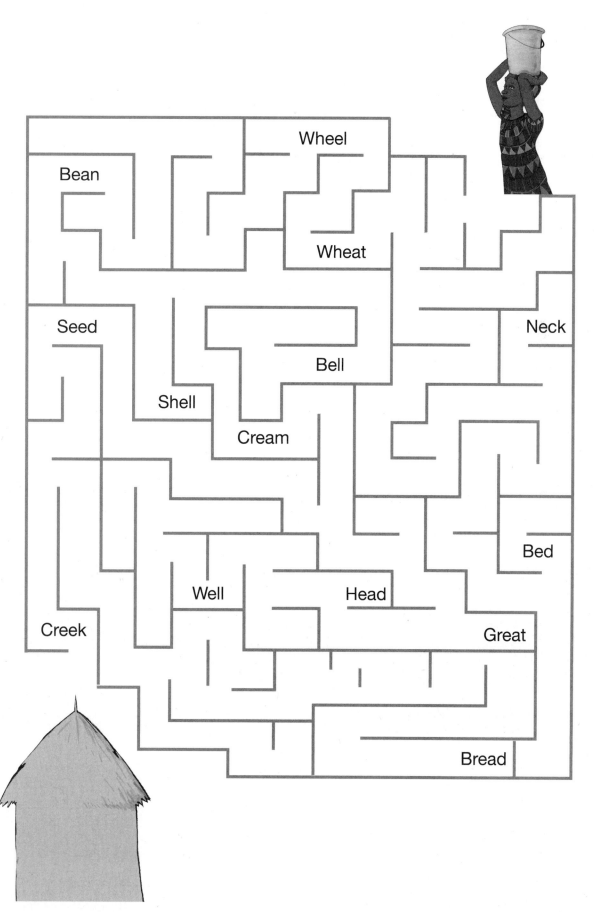

Bean

Wheel

Wheat

Seed

Neck

Bell

Shell

Cream

Bed

Well

Head

Creek

Great

Bread

1. I felt _____ riding on the ship. (seasick, sleep)

2. Can you _____ me how to drive? (reach, teach)

3. My sister made me _____. (steam, scream)

4. Could I _____ have a slice of cake? (Pete, please)

5. The _____ fall off the tree in the fall. (leaves, trees)

6. A _____ is a bird with a tail like a fan. (peacock, eagle)

7. The toy will squeak when you _____ it. (squeeze, leave)

8. I like a _____ treat after school. (sweet, steam)

9. I have _____ sisters. (three, tree)

10. "Bless you," he said when I _____. (sneezed, reached)

11. I like to read the tale, "Sheep in a _____." (Jeep, Leave)

12. _____ was a bad man in *The Frog Race*. (Steve, Pete)

The snake was sitting on a rock in the sun. It had red stripes and black stripes on its skin. The scales on the snake's skin glinted in the sunshine. The snake got nice and hot in the sun. The snake will catch mice for a snack. It is good for a snake to munch on mice. When the snake gets big, the snake will shed its skin. When the sun sets and it is bed time, the snake will be safe hiding in the sand.

Directions: Have students draw a picture illustrating the text read in the paragraph.

| owl | now | out | shout | cow |
| mouse | howl | brown | frown | trout |

Across

3. A fish

4. not a smile

6. a loud voice

9. a bird

10. "Go to bed _____," said Mom.

Down

1. One _____, two mice

2. How now, _____ cow

5. not inside but ____side

7. A dog will _____ at the moon.

8. "Moo," said the _____.

Directions: Read the clues to the students and guide the completion of the crossword puzzle.

Directions: Help the cow find the best flowers to eat. Color only the flowers with the /ou/ sound.

shower

allowed

powder

brown

grump

hare

too

rabbit

panther

town

batboy	toybox	toys	coiled
soil	boiling	coins	

1. The sun is _____ hot outside.

2. Did you see the snake all _____ up?

3. The _____ will keep the baseball bats neat.

4. We will plant the seeds in the _____.

5. Pick up the toys and place them in the _____.

6. Could you help me count my _____?

7. Are the stuffed _____ on the bed?

Directions: Students should read the sentences and fill in the blank with the best word.

'oy' = blue

'oi' = green

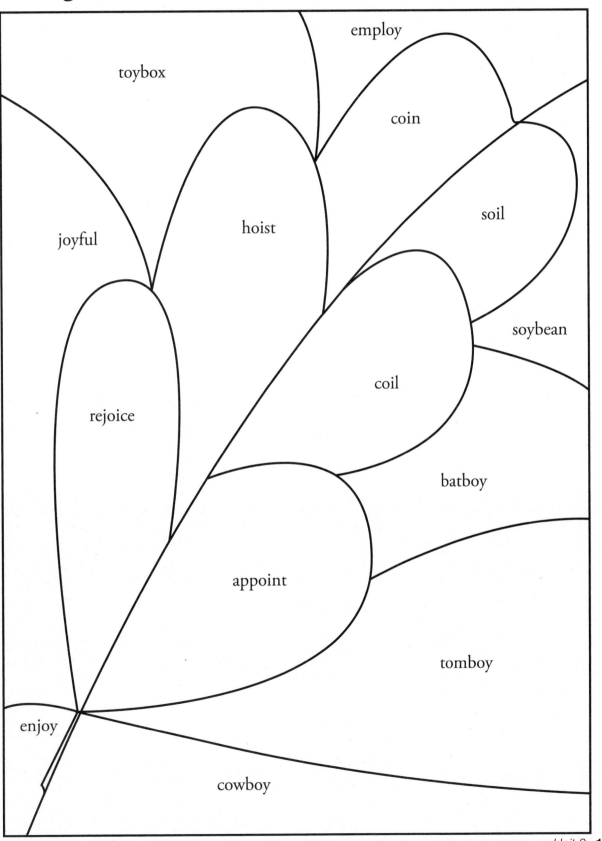

employ

toybox

coin

joyful

hoist

soil

soybean

rejoice

coil

batboy

appoint

tomboy

enjoy

cowboy

'er'

after	sister	marker	chapter
herd	fern	perch	number

Directions: Have students choose the correct word that fits best in the sentence. After writing the word in the blank, have him or her circle the 'er' spelling.

1. Ten is the _____ I like best.

2. The _____ of cows ate grass.

3. Do you have the red _____?

4. The green _____ needs water and sun.

5. My big _____, Jan, is tall.

6. The bird is sleeping on its _____.

7. _____class, I like to take a nap.

8. That _____ of the book was long.

'or' and 'ar'

arm	shark	farmer	car	torn
corn	yarn	cart	thorn	

Directions: Have students choose the best word to complete the sentence. After writing the word in the blank, have him or her circle either the 'or' or 'ar' spelling.

1. The red _____ went down the street fast.

2. Mark has a cut on his _____.

3. Do you like to eat _____ in the summer?

4. The _____ had pigs and cows on his land.

5. Did he place the food in his shopping _____?

6. The _____ on the rose was sharp.

7. My mom uses _____ when she knits.

8. That is a big _____ in the sea!

9. His shirt was ripped and _____.

'or', 'er', and 'ar'

north	letter	garlic	morning	better
car	porch	cartoon	ladder	swimmer
short	far	river	form	garden

/er/ as in *her*	/ar/ as in *car*	/or/ as in *for*

Directions: Have students read each word aloud, write the word under the correct header, and circle the /or/, /er/, or /ar/.

'or,' 'ar,' and 'er'

north	letter	garlic	morning	better
car	porch	cartoon	ladder	swimmer
short	far	river	form	garden

Directions: Have students select words from the box and use them to write sentences.

1. _____

2. _____

3. _____

4. _____

5. _____

Print the words in the box on the lines where they fit best.

artist	barefoot	tadpole
~~duckling~~	comics	checkers

duckling _____ _____

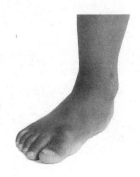

_____ _____ _____

| bookcase | broomstick | dentist |
| fireplace | handshake | iceberg |

_____   _____   _____

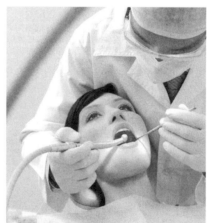

_____   _____   _____

Directions: Read these words with your students. Ask them to "horseshoe circle" the pattern at the top of the column.

a_e	i_e
cupcake	sunshine
pancake	reptile
mistake	sunrise
fateful	timeline
bracelet	inside
cascade	pastime
snakeskin	combine
inflate	subscribe
translate	hostile

Print the words on the lines where they fit the best.

1. winter

_____   winter   _____

2. river

_____   _____   _____

3. forest

_____   _____   _____

4. farmer

5. ladder

6. collar

Name _____

Print the words in the box on the lines where they fit the best.

| children | ~~number~~ | winter |
| kitchen | garden | fingers |

<u>number</u> _____ _____

_____ _____ _____

writing	coffee	pocket
fireplace	fifteen	soccer

15

_____ _____ _____

 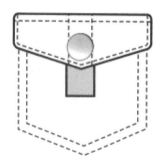 

_____ _____ _____

1. _____   1. _____

2. _____   2. _____

3. _____   3. _____

4. _____   4. _____

5. _____   5. _____

6. _____   6. _____

7. _____   7. _____

8. _____   8. _____

9. _____   9. _____

10. _____   10. _____

Directions: Have students practice writing the Tricky Words listed in the Teacher Guide.

Print *yes* or *no* on the lines.

1. Can a mule cook dinner? _____ no _____

2. Can you wave your hand? _____

3. Are your feet green? _____

4. Can you swim in a pool? _____

5. Is a dime less than a nickel? _____

6. Is a river wet? _____

7. Is it dark at noon? _____

8. Is a cake sweet? _____

9. Are there cats on the moon? _____

10. Can a rock swim? _____

11. Is a boiling pot hot? _____

12. Is butter red? _____

Print *yes* or *no* on the lines.

1. Can a pepper be green?   _yes_

2. Do pigs moo?   _____

3. Is ice hot?   _____

4. Can you use a pen to write?   _____

5. Do words have letters?   _____

6. Can a fish oink?   _____

7. Is nineteen a number? _____

8. Is it hot at the South Pole? _____

9. Do fish have feet? _____

10. Is shouting loud? _____

11. Is a panther a fish? _____

12. Do raccoons have fins? _____

Check the sentence that is the best fit.

1.  ☑ Roses have thorns.
   ☐ Roses have horns.

2.  ☐ My house has a yard.
   ☐ My cloud has a yard.

3.  ☐ I can knit mittens.
   ☐ I can knit kittens.

4.  ☐ Dentists fix teeth.
   ☐ Dentists fix sheep.

5.  ☐ This pup is cute.
   ☐ This duck is cute.

6.  ☐ I swim in the pool.
   ☐ I run on the moon.

7.

☐ Trees are green.

☐ Bees are green.

8.

☐ He rides a bike.

☐ He rides a horse.

9.

☐ I have a dime.

☐ I have a lime.

10.

☐ The band is loud.

☐ The fan is loud.

11.

☐ This is a good book.

☐ He is a good cook.

12.

☐ The artist can paint.

☐ The artist can faint.

drop	ask	shrug	slump	limp
yank	plop	like	pat	yell

Directions: Ask students to use one word from the box in each sentence. He or she will need to add –ed to each word.

1. "Zip! Zing!" he _____. "Take that, T. Rex!"

2. He _____ back the drapes.

3. "Ug!" Mike said. He _____ and _____ his chin on his chest.

4. "What if I tell you a bedtime tale?" he _____.

5. Mike did not think it would help much. He _____.

6. "When I was a kid, your gramp would tell me bedtime tales. I _____ them."

7. Mike's dad sat down on the bed and _____ Mike on the back of the neck.

8. Mike _____ to his bed and _____ down on it.

dent	melt	jot	rub	beg
jog	hop	hope	tape	tap

1. Someone _____ me on the head.

2. The dog _____ for a treat.

3. I _____ my hands together.

4. The side of the truck was _____ in the wreck.

5. My candy _____ when I left it in the sun.

6. Mom _____ down a list for shopping.

7. He _____ like a rabbit.

8. Dad _____ down the street.

9. We _____ to get a gift from Gramps.

10. She _____ the poster to the wall.

Directions: Ask students to add -ing to each word. Then write the correct word in the blank for the sentence on the next page.

smile _____

race _____

bake _____

invite _____

confuse _____

taste _____

compete _____

hop _____

1. Can we make the _____ car go faster?

2. Are you _____ all of us to your picnic?

3. Dad is _____ cake for my snack.

4. I like _____ the frosting for the cake.

5. We were glad and _____ when we left the park.

6. It was _____ to see the twins.

7. The frogs were _____ in the race.

8. The frog was _____ to the pond.

Directions: Ask students to look in the Reader and copy exactly the words that the character said on the blanks below the character's picture. Students should be told that they will need to be able to read the quotes aloud to the class or to a family member using the character's voice.

_____

_____

_____

_____

_____

_____

_____

_____

_____

_____

_____

_____

_____

_____

Directions: Ask students to look in the Reader and copy exactly the words that the character said on the blanks below the character's picture. Students should be told that they will need to be able to read the quotes aloud to the class or to a family member using the character's voice.

_____

_____

_____

_____

_____

_____

_____

_____

_____

_____

_____

_____

Directions: Ask students to look in the Reader and copy exactly the words that the character said on the blanks below the character's picture. Students should be told that they will need to be able to read the quotes aloud to the class or to a family member using the character's voice.

_____

_____

_____

_____

_____

_____

_____

_____

_____

_____

_____

Big Jim's frog looks like _____   My pet looks like _____
_____   _____
_____   _____
_____   _____

Big Jim's frog likes to _____   My pet likes to _____
_____   _____
_____   _____
_____   _____

Big Jim's frog likes to eat _____   My pet likes to eat _____
_____   _____
_____   _____
_____   _____

Big Jim's frog can _____   My pet can _____
_____   _____
_____   _____
_____   _____

Title:

Characters

Setting

Directions: Complete the worksheet on any story from Bedtime Tales.

Plot

Beginning

Middle

End

Title of Book: _____

Author: _____

Characters: _____

_____

What happened?

_____
_____
_____
_____
_____
_____
_____
_____
_____
_____
_____
_____
_____
_____

How did it end?

_____
_____
_____
_____
_____

Directions: Have students select any story from the Reader to complete the book report.

How to make a pancake

1. You will need:

   _____

   _____

   _____

   _____

2. Then you mix together _____

   _____

   _____

   _____

3. Then _____

   _____

   _____

4. Then you cook it for _____

   _____

   _____

   _____

Directions: In "The Pancake," Mom makes a pancake. Have students write a recipe for making a pancake and draw a picture to go with it.

CORE KNOWLEDGE LANGUAGE ARTS

SERIES EDITOR-IN-CHIEF
E. D. Hirsch, Jr.

PRESIDENT
Linda Bevilacqua

EDITORIAL STAFF
Carolyn Gosse, Senior Editor - Preschool
Khara Turnbull, Materials Development Manager
Michelle L. Warner, Senior Editor - Listening & Learning

Mick Anderson
Robin Blackshire
Maggie Buchanan
Paula Coyner
Sue Fulton
Sara Hunt
Erin Kist
Robin Luecke
Rosie McCormick
Cynthia Peng
Liz Pettit
Ellen Sadler
Deborah Samley
Diane Auger Smith
Sarah Zelinke

DESIGN AND GRAPHICS STAFF
Scott Ritchie, Creative Director

Kim Berrall
Michael Donegan
Liza Greene
Matt Leech
Bridget Moriarty
Lauren Pack

CONSULTING PROJECT MANAGEMENT SERVICES
ScribeConcepts.com

ADDITIONAL CONSULTING SERVICES
Ang Blanchette
Dorrit Green
Carolyn Pinkerton

ACKNOWLEDGMENTS

These materials are the result of the work, advice, and encouragement of numerous individuals over many years. Some of those singled out here already know the depth of our gratitude; others may be surprised to find themselves thanked publicly for help they gave quietly and generously for the sake of the enterprise alone. To helpers named and unnamed we are deeply grateful.

CONTRIBUTORS TO EARLIER VERSIONS OF THESE MATERIALS
Susan B. Albaugh, Kazuko Ashizawa, Nancy Braier, Kathryn M. Cummings, Michelle De Groot, Diana Espinal, Mary E. Forbes, Michael L. Ford, Ted Hirsch, Danielle Knecht, James K. Lee, Diane Henry Leipzig, Martha G. Mack, Liana Mahoney, Isabel McLean, Steve Morrison, Juliane K. Munson, Elizabeth B. Rasmussen, Laura Tortorelli, Rachael L. Shaw, Sivan B. Sherman, Miriam E. Vidaver, Catherine S. Whittington, Jeannette A. Williams

We would like to extend special recognition to Program Directors Matthew Davis and Souzanne Wright who were instrumental to the early development of this program.

SCHOOLS
We are truly grateful to the teachers, students, and administrators of the following schools for their willingness to field test these materials and for their invaluable advice: Capitol View Elementary, Challenge Foundation Academy (IN), Community Academy Public Charter School, Lake Lure Classical Academy, Lepanto Elementary School, New Holland Core Knowledge Academy, Paramount School of Excellence, Pioneer Challenge Foundation Academy, New York City PS 26R (The Carteret School), PS 30X (Wilton School), PS 50X (Clara Barton School), PS 96Q, PS 102X (Joseph O. Loretan), PS 104Q (The Bays Water), PS 214K (Michael Friedsam), PS 223Q (Lyndon B. Johnson School), PS 308K (Clara Cardwell), PS 333Q (Goldie Maple Academy), Sequoyah Elementary School, South Shore Charter Public School, Spartanburg Charter School, Steed Elementary School, Thomas Jefferson Classical Academy, Three Oaks Elementary, West Manor Elementary.

And a special thanks to the CKLA Pilot Coordinators Anita Henderson, Yasmin Lugo-Hernandez, and Susan Smith, whose suggestions and day-to-day support to teachers using these materials in their classrooms was critical.